# Dinosaurs
# and the
# Bible

Ralph O. Muncaster

HARVEST HOUSE™ PUBLISHERS

EUGENE, OREGON

*Cover by Terry Dugan Design, Minneapolis, Minnesota*

*Cover photo © The Field Museum, #GEO85827c*

*Dinosaur illustrations by Matt Shoemaker. Not intended for scientific purposes.*

*Photo on page 9 used by courtesy of Charles Dean Pruitt and the Mathematical Foundation. For more information about the Mathematical Foundation, visit their Web site at www.mathematical.com.*

## DINOSAURS AND THE BIBLE

Examine the Evidence™ Series
Copyright © 2003 by Ralph O. Muncaster
Published by Harvest House Publishers
Eugene, Oregon 97402

Harvest House Publishers, Inc., is the exclusive licensee of the trademark EXAMINE THE EVIDENCE.

Library of Congress Cataloging-in-Publication Data

Muncaster, Ralph O.
    Dinosaurs and the Bible / Ralph O. Muncaster.
        p. cm. — (Examine the evidence)
    Includes bibliographical references.
    ISBN 0-7369-0906-0 (pbk.)
    1. Bible—Evidences, authority, etc.  I. Title.
    BS480.M747 2003
    220.8'5679—dc21                                    2003001997

06  07  08  09  / BP-MS /  10  9  8  7  6  5  4  3  2

# Contents

# The Great Mystery

The first rays of sunlight slice through the mist that hovers over the lush forests and swampland. Almost as if on cue, the head of the brachiosaurus arches gracefully, rising 40 feet skyward as it surveys the landscape below. Slowly, the magnificent creature lumbers through the forest. Each step of the 80-ton reptile causes the ground to quake, as it crushes everything underneath its feet.

As daybreak in the world of the dinosaurs continues, the great winged quetzalcoatlus leaves its roost to glide over the surface of the surf in search of the morning's catch of fish and crabs. Dog-sized eoraptors scurry about on their hind legs, searching for a quick meal or, better yet, hoping to feast on someone else's leftovers. An enormous, tanklike ankylosaurus, covered with large bony plates, moves slowly over the ground like a lawnmower, gathering as much low-lying plant life as possible to satisfy its huge daily appetite. A triceratops chews peacefully on its morning meal of small plants.

Suddenly a tyrannosaurus thunders through the brush, causing all creatures in the vicinity to scatter. The triceratops can't escape, and jaws of death rip into its hide. A ferocious battle ensues. Ultimately the tearing teeth and bone-crushing bites of the T. rex prove too much for it, and the triceratops succumbs as yet another victim.

Dinosaurs are a fascinating mystery of times past.

The world of dinosaurs is too big to ignore. So we might ask, were dinosaurs included in the Bible? If so, where? And if not, why?

# The Key Issues

## 1. Are Dinosaurs in the Bible?

Such enormous and dominant creatures would command recognition—even in the Bible, though it focuses on people's relationship with God, not zoology. Like all other creatures, dinosaurs must have been created by God. So where, if anywhere, can we find them in the Bible?

(Pages 30–41)

## 2. Did Dinosaurs Coexist with Humans?

Genesis describes six "days" of creation. This seems to imply that dinosaurs coexisted with humans. However, the generally accepted scientific viewpoint is that dinosaurs were long extinct by the time people arrived. How can this contradiction be reconciled?

(Pages 20–27)

## 3. What Role Did Dinosaurs Play in God's Creation?

Can we ever understand the reason for the existence of the many species of dinosaurs? Has their existence affected our world today?

(Pages 42–43)

# Dinosaurs in Ancient Art and Writing

No creatures have captured the imagination of people like dinosaurs, even though we now have only silent fossilized skeletons to testify to them. And this human fascination with them seems to have existed for thousands of years.

People today have a tendency to think of *paleontology*—the study of past geological eras through fossils—as only a modern science. They rarely consider the possibility that ancient people may have engaged in such activity as well. Although the quantity and quality of research has improved in modern times, there is considerable evidence that ancient people also uncovered fossilized bones and attempted to discern their origin and meaning. Often the explanations they created based on their findings developed into myths or into attempts to corroborate the myths that already exsited at the time. Apart from this, in many respects ancient paleontology was similar to today's. Evidence indicates that, as far back as 2000 B.C., dinosaur bones were considered to have originated long before then.

## Ancient Heroes

Dinosaur-like creatures are often depicted on vases, paintings, jewelry, and other items from ancient Greece, Rome, and Egypt. Occasionally, the artwork is very accurate in its representation of certain dinosaurs. Some believe that this is evidence that dinosaurs were still roaming about at that time. Others say no. But if this detailed artwork was not conceived from living dinosaurs, where did the ideas come from?

As already mentioned, ancient civilizations had more involvement in paleontology than we generally imagine. The entire Mediterranean region is rich in fossils. Earthquakes, landslides, erosion, and excavation exposed layers of rock, and large bones from past ages would suddenly be found by unsuspecting people. Some of the fossilized bones that would commonly be seen were those of the *Palaeoloxodon antiquus* (a type of dinosaur elephant), the grotesque ancylotherium (a lumbering herbivore with hooked claws), the *Mammuthus primigenius* (the wooly mammoth), and ancient rhinoceroses and mastodons.

## Fossilized Bones Were Valued

Ancient people apparently often believed that dinosaur bones were actually the bones of ancient mythological heroes. The bones were placed in temples and other places of honor, where they were revered by worshipers. In many cases, these special, venerated bones were written about by historians of the day—for example, it was reported that sometimes dinosaur bones had been placed in coffins and buried as if they were those of a human hero. Competing cities would even use such fossilized bones to suggest that their ancestral heroes were superior to those of other cities, and occasionally there were skirmishes over the rights to those ancient fossil remnants.

Sometimes dinosaur fossils were rearranged to create enormous human-appearing "heroes." Fossilized elephants and mammoths have been found—tusks missing—buried in coffins and arranged to look human. In Egypt, between 1300 and 1200 B.C., some three tons of black, river-polished fossilized bones were placed in shrines, where they were worshiped and reburied as relics of Set, the god of darkness. Most of these bones were from fossilized hippopotamuses or extinct crocodiles (see pages 34–38).

In the Mediterranean region, the eighth and seventh centuries B.C. were particularly active times of collecting of "cult fossils," which were often gathered to honor gods of mythology. The hero–gods Achilles and Ajax are among the many to whom fossilized bones were attributed. Ancient writing dating as far back as 440 B.C. confirm the existence of many such "fossil-heroes."[1]

### A Holy Relic

In A.D. 150, the Greek historian Pausanias wrote about a large shoulder bone that had been venerated since the time of the Trojan War (about 1250 B.C.). A seer had told the Greek army that, in order for the city of Troy to fall, an ancient, mystical shoulder-blade bone had to be retrieved from its shrine on

Mount Olympus. According to the legend, the bone had turned to ivory in ages past—and it even had its own shrine in the temple of Artemis on Mount Olympus, where it had been kept in a bronze chest for many years.

In reality, the bone was from the shoulder of an ancient mammoth. It was mistakenly thought to be ivory because the minerals that caused fossilization in that region had created a white sheen on its surface.

## Ancient Monsters

In other cases more complete skeletons of ancient dinosaurs were pieced together to provide an idea of what ancient non-human creatures looked like (see the following insert about the griffin). Sets of extinct crocodile bones combined with fossilized heads of extinct giraffes are believed to have led to descriptions of dragons by the people of the Mediterranean region. For instance, when the Greek historian Herodotus journeyed to Egypt, he heard tales of giant flying reptiles or dragons. Later he returned in search of the creatures and discovered large numbers of ancient bones that had been collected and piled in heaps inside shrines.

Even Roman emperors were fascinated by the mystery of the fossils. Tiberius (42 B.C.–A.D. 37, emperor at the time of Jesus' ministry—see Luke 1:1) spent his boyhood in Sparta, Greece, where many fossils were uncovered. Later, as emperor, he received reports of remains of monsters from historians such as Pliny. Fascinated by such reports, Tiberius took an active interest in the finds and even retired to the island of Capri, which was the site of a large paleontological museum founded by the emperor Augustus.

In short, paleontology was flourishing in the ancient Mediterranean world. But in spite of this interest, there is no written record of *living* dinosaurs from any civilization—though, as we've seen, there are many written records of bones that are attributed to ancient mythological heroes and monsters. And as far as the myths themselves (such as Homer's *Iliad*), they were clearly not intended to be history.

## The Myth of the Griffins

Griffins are depicted in much ancient artwork and literature. Legends were widespread throughout the Mediterranean area about these fierce creatures that roamed the gold-laden land of Scythia (Central Asia east of the Black Sea), ferociously protecting its treasure from the many gold-seekers. Supposedly, griffins would sometimes hoard gold or gems in their nests. Although no records indicate that anyone had ever actually seen a griffin, the descriptions were very consistent. Griffins were envisioned as similar to a large lion, with a birdlike, beaked head. Many griffins were described as having wings and a pointed, demon-like tail. Their skin was described in several different ways—sometimes furry, sometimes leathery, sometimes feathery.

Further, Ctesias, a Greek historian of the fifth century B.C., described griffins as a "race of four-legged birds." If no griffins had ever been seen, what did he base this description on? Where did the other ideas about griffins' appearance come from? The Gobi Desert in Central Asia provides some clues. The Gobi contains many of the most common and well-preserved fossils in the world. Even today, the shifting sands of the desert frequently reveal ancient bones that have weathered to the surface, where they are discovered by passersby. No doubt the same thing occurred in ancient times.

One of the most common fossils in the region is that of the *protoceratops*. The head of the protoceratops has a fierce-looking beak-like feature; large, threatening eye sockets; and a hatchet-shaped face, with bones protruding from the back of its head. In addition, this creature is four-legged, is roughly the size of a lion, and has a bony spine that runs down its back.

*Photo courtesy of Charles Dean Pruitt and the Mathematical Foundation.*

In short, all the criteria for a griffin are met. In all likelihood, ancient gold-seekers who discovered this fossil created tales about the creature that the bones represented in an attempt to scare others away from their finds—and the legend of the griffin was born.

# Dinosaurs, Dinosaurs—
# Classifications and Examples

The word "dinosaur" literally means "terrifying lizard." Today we have millions of dinosaur fossils, which provide us with an accurate record of the many types of dinosaurs, along with a glimpse of the lifestyle of each. Dinosaurs make up two of the six classifications of reptiles. Here's a chart to illustrate this relationship.

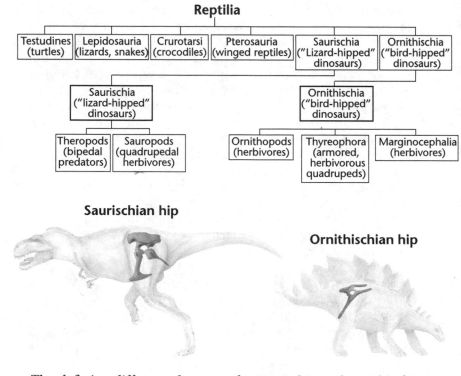

**Saurischian hip**

**Ornithischian hip**

The defining difference between the saurischia and ornithischia dinosaur orders is in hip structure. Oddly enough, the names seem to be reversed. Saurischia, or "lizard-hipped" dinosaurs, have a hip structure that is similar to that of lizards, yet many of them apparently walked upright like birds. On the other hand, the ornithischia, or "bird-hipped" dinosaurs, generally walked on all fours like lizards, yet they have a hip structure that is similar to birds.

## Saurischian Dinosaurs

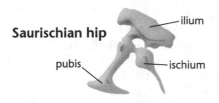

**Saurischian hip**

In the hips of saurischian dinosaurs, the pubis bone points downward and forward like a lizard's hip. Saurischia are broken down into the *theropods* and *sauropods*.

### Theropods

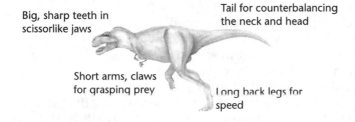

Theropods were carnivorous (meat-eating) dinosaurs that had sharp, slicing teeth and strong jaw muscles. They walked on two feet and were especially fast and agile, with strong legs and clawed, birdlike feet, as well as large eye sockets, which may indicate good eyesight. Here are a few examples of theropods:

- *Eoraptor* ("dawn thief"): A small dinosaur, standing only about 3 feet high. It was fast and ran on its hind legs to catch prey in its small sharp teeth. The eoraptor may have also been a scavenger. Each of its hands had five fingers—two of which were small. The eoraptor was found in southern Argentina and is believed to be one of the earliest dinosaurs.

- *Baryonyx* ("heavy claw"): A highly unusual dinosaur that was about 32 feet long and may have weighed as much as 2 tons. Its unusually long crocodile-like snout had a small crest and contained 96 serrated teeth. Its head was supported by a long neck. It ate fish, as evidenced by fossilized fish remains that have been found along with its fossils.

  It's unclear whether the baryonyx walked on two legs only or on all fours. All its legs were heavy and muscular, and the front legs were only slightly smaller than the hind ones. It is believed to have waded in rivers and shallow seas to catch fish, as some modern bears do.

- *Spinosaurus* ("spiny lizard"): A huge dinosaur, 40 to 50 feet long and weighing about 8 tons. It was characterized by a large sail-like fin that towered six feet over its back, and it had a flexible spine that allowed it to spread this fin much like a fan. The fin may have been used for temperature regulation and possibly also for a mating ritual. The spinosaurus was an aggressive meat-eating dinosaur with sharp crocodile-like teeth, and it fed on large fish and other dinosaurs.

- *Tyrannosaurus rex* ("tyrant lizard king"): Perhaps the most famous dinosaur. This theropod is known as perhaps the most ferocious land creature that ever lived. It was the biggest known carnivore, reaching a length of about 40 feet, a height of 15 to 20 feet, and a weight of 5 to 7 tons.

  The tyrannosaurus had a huge head with powerful, 4-foot jaws containing sharp, replaceable teeth that were some 9 inches in length. (One fossilized tooth was found to be 13 inches long!) It is no wonder it is regarded as the most fearsome creature that ever lived. It was literally a "devouring machine" and could consume 500 pounds of meat in one single bite, its prey being mostly plant-eating dinosaurs.

Each of the tyrannosaurus's tiny arms had a birdlike foot with three claws. Running on its hind legs with a pointed tail for balance and able to make quick turns, the T. rex had a stride of some 12 to 15 feet and could run about 15 mph—nearly as fast as the fastest human sprinters. What a horrifying creature this enormous, fast, agile, meat-eating predator must have been.

## Sauropods

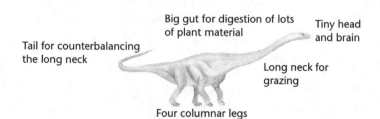

Big gut for digestion of lots of plant material

Tiny head and brain

Tail for counterbalancing the long neck

Long neck for grazing

Four columnar legs

Sauropods were large herbivores (plant-eaters). They had small heads with small brains, attached to long slender necks for grazing, and consumed vast amounts of plants daily. These creatures walked slowly on four large, columnlike legs. They were the largest land animals that ever lived. Following are a few examples of sauropods:

- *Brachiosaurus* ("arm lizard"): One of the largest and tallest living creatures ever found. It had a length of about 85 feet, stood 40 feet tall, and weighed anywhere from 33 to 88 tons. Its long, slender neck and small head were counterbalanced by a long, slender tail. It lived on land (not in swamps, as originally thought) and ate the tops of trees. Food was eaten whole and broken down entirely in the stomach. The brachiosaurus probably traveled in herds and migrated when the food supply dwindled. It is believed that it had a life span of more than 100 years.

- *Amargasaurus* ("lizard from La Amarga [Argentina]"): A 33-foot-long plant-eater with two rows of spines protruding from its back. These spines were used as a thermoregulatory device and probably also had a role in mating rituals. Although the front legs of the amargasaurus were slightly smaller than its back ones, each of its feet had five elephant-like toes, one of which contained a sharp claw for protection. This dinosaur also had a whiplike tail that could be used for protection. Like other sauropods, the amargasaurus probably hatched from eggs, traveled in herds, ate conifers, and lived to be about 100 years old.

- *Diplodocus* ("double-beamed"): One of the longest creatures that ever existed. It was about 90 feet long, with a 26-foot neck and a 45-foot tail. The nostrils of the diplodocus were located on the top of its small head, and its teeth were located only in the front of its mouth. It had elephant-like feet with five toes—one toe larger and with a sharp claw (like the amargasaurus), probably used for protection. Extra bones under the backbone of this dinosaur acted as "double beams" for support and possibly enabled a sharp, whiplike action of the creature's tail. It has been determined that this dinosaur could not lift its head above about 17 feet.

# Ornithischian Dinosaurs

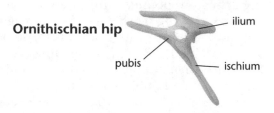

**Ornithischian hip**

ilium

pubis

ischium

The ornithischian dinosaurs had a hip structure that pointed down and toward the tail. Ornithischia are divided into *ornithopods, thyreophora,* and *marginocephalia.*

## Ornithopods

"Ornithopod" literally means "bird foot." These dinosaurs walked on two legs, but had no body armor. They varied greatly in size and appearance. Some were small and fast, while others were large and cumbersome. Although all had a beak of some sort, in many cases it was more like a duck bill. Many of these dinosaurs had some form of head crest. Some of the best-known ornithopods include the following:

- *Corythosaurus* ("helmet lizard"): A large duck-billed dinosaur that grew to be about 33 feet long and 6 feet tall, and weighed up to 5 tons. It was a plant-eater and had a characteristic helmet crest on its head. Scientists have speculated on the purpose of the crest. Some believe it was a thermoradiator to help maintain proper temperature. Others believe it enhanced the creature's sense of smell since the part of its brain that sensed smell was located in the crest. Still others believe that its primary purpose was in mating displays.

  The corythosaurus had no teeth, and consequently ground its food before swallowing. These dinosaurs traveled in herds and are believed to have lived primarily along shorelines, perhaps moving to higher ground to reproduce.

- *Hypsilophodon* ("high-crested tooth"): About 6 feet long, 2 feet tall, and weighing about 150 pounds. This dinosaur had a stiff tail and slender legs, making it relatively fast and agile as it ran on its hind feet. Its beak was made of horn and contained 28 self-sharpening teeth for chewing plants. Its small upper arms had five-fingered hands, although its feet had only four toes.

  The hypsilophodon was a herd animal. In one location, 20 fossils were found buried together. Nests of carefully placed eggs have been found that indicate that this dinosaur may have cared for its young, at least initially.

- *Ouranosaurus* ("brave lizard"): A sail-backed plant-eater that grew to a length of 23 feet and a weight of about 4 tons. The characteristic sail on its back was used for temperature regulation in the hot African climate. It dispersed extra heat when the sail was turned away from the sun and collected heat when it faced the sun. The ouranosaurus could move on either two or four legs, but it was a bulky, slow-moving dinosaur.

## Thyreophora

Thyreophora (literally, "shield-bearers") were large, four-legged dinosaurs that fell into two basic categories: stegosauria—dinosaurs with armor; and ankylosauria—dinosaurs with plates. These well-protected dinosaurs were very cumbersome and slow-moving. Examples of these herbivorous dinosaurs include the following:

- *Ankylosaurus* ("crooked lizard"): A huge, lumbering dinosaur that measured 25 to 35 feet long and weighed 3 to 4 tons. It was covered with thick oval protective plates that were embedded in its leathery skin. Two rows of spikes ran along the length of its back, and large spikes protruded from its head and the back of its clublike tail. It walked on four stubby legs and had a short neck supporting a wide head, which contained a tiny brain.

The ankylosaurus was an extremely heavy reptile and, because of its size, needed to consume great amounts of plants daily. Scientists believe it had a fermentation compartment in its gut to assist it in digestion of food. It was well-protected from predators and was virtually impossible to overcome unless it was flipped over.

- *Stegosaurus* ("covered lizard"): A dinosaur that grew up to a length of 25 to 30 feet, a height of 9 feet, and a weight of about 3½ tons. It had 17 large, flat, bony triangular plates that alternated from side to side along its spine, and a heavy spiked tail for protection. Its skull was long, pointed, and narrow, and its mouth had only small teeth, in the cheeks. Its brain was small—about the size of a walnut.

The triangular plates along the back of the stegosaurus contained tube-like tunnels, indicating they were nourished by blood vessels—possibly because they were used for temperature control. Other armorlike plates covered the sides of its neck, its pelvic area, and the sides of some species. The tail spikes grew to a length of 4 feet and offered protection against large meat-eating dinosaurs. The stegosaurus ate large quantities of plants, and though it generally walked on all fours, it would probably also rear up on its hind legs from time to time to reach higher bushes.

## Marginocephalia

"Marginocephalia" literally means "fringed head." These dinosaurs were characterized by a distinctive skull structure with a "shelf" or "frill" on the back of the skull, though some of these plant-eaters simply had a thickened skull structure. Some moved about on four feet, while others walked upright. Here are some examples of marginocephalia:

- *Triceratops* ("three-horned face"): A well-known dinosaur, similar to today's rhinoceros. It walked on four massive legs and had three large horns protruding from a

platelike structure covering its head. The head of the triceratops is one of the largest of any creature, measuring some 10 feet in length—about a third of the size of its body, which grew up to 30 feet in length and about 10 feet in height, and weighed from 6 to 12 tons.

Evidence from several beds of triceratops fossils indicates that it was a herd dinosaur. Its horns offered significant protection from predators, and it is believed that the triceratops charged its enemies in the same way a rhino charges its enemies today.

- *Pachycephalosaurus* ("thick-headed lizard"): A dome-headed dinosaur with an incredibly thick skull—up to 10 inches thick. This skull contained a small brain and housed large eyes, as well as having bumpy knobs at the snout and around its back.

The pachycephalosaurus grew to about 15 feet in length, with a weight of about a half-ton. It was a plant-eater that walked on its hind feet, using its stiff tail for balance. It apparently lived in small groups in coastal regions and probably used its speed to escape from its enemies.

## Dinosaurs with Humans?

A few years ago, several articles were published with "exciting news"—that fossilized human footprints had been discovered alongside dinosaur footprints dating from the same time in the limestone beds along the Paluxy River in Glen Rose, Texas. This was initially thought to be good evidence that dinosaurs and human beings had roamed the earth together.

More in-depth analysis by experts, and eventually by even the authors of the articles themselves, revealed—to the embarrassment of many—that *all* of the footprints were from dinosaurs. There were no human footprints.[2] Unfortunately, many Web sites and articles still cite the previous, incorrect information.

In regard to the dinosaur timeline, it is wise not to rush to conclusions and later be forced to recant. For non-Christians, this can call into question other evidence, already well-established, that does support the Bible. The Glen Rose fossil beds are a case in point.

# The Great Time Issue

When did the dinosaurs roam the earth? The vast body of scientific evidence points to the conclusion that the dinosaur age lasted from about 248 million years ago to about 65 million years ago. Many scientists also believe that human beings didn't appear on the earth until—very approximately—about 40,000 years ago. (Definitions of which creatures were actually human vary.) Thus, the majority of scientists believe that dinosaurs were long extinct when mankind appeared.

Others believe that a strict and careful interpretation of the Bible seems to indicate that everything was created in six literal days. This, when combined with the genealogies listed in the Scriptures, implies that human beings and dinosaurs coexisted at a time only 6,000 to 10,000 years ago. Here's a timeline contrast of the two views:

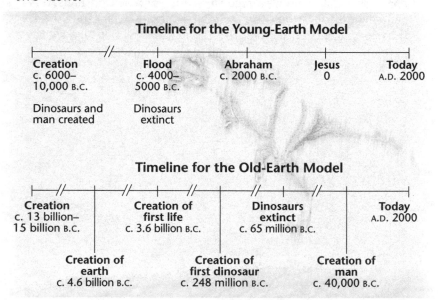

### Timeline for the Young-Earth Model

| Creation<br>c. 6000–<br>10,000 B.C. | Flood<br>c. 4000–<br>5000 B.C. | Abraham<br>c. 2000 B.C. | Jesus<br>0 | Today<br>A.D. 2000 |
| --- | --- | --- | --- | --- |
| Dinosaurs and<br>man created | Dinosaurs<br>extinct | | | |

### Timeline for the Old-Earth Model

| Creation<br>c. 13 billion–<br>15 billion B.C. | | Creation of<br>first life<br>c. 3.6 billion B.C. | | Dinosaurs<br>extinct<br>c. 65 million B.C. | | Today<br>A.D. 2000 |
| --- | --- | --- | --- | --- | --- | --- |
| | Creation of<br>earth<br>c. 4.6 billion B.C. | | Creation of<br>first dinosaur<br>c. 248 million B.C. | | Creation of<br>man<br>c. 40,000 B.C. | |

## The Young-Earth Viewpoint

This view holds that the age of the earth is only 6,000 to 10,000 years, based on the account of creation in the book of Genesis and a reconstruction of the many genealogies in the Bible.

Of particular importance are the six "days" of creation in Genesis 1. The young-earth viewpoint believes that the original Hebrew word *yom*—translated as "day" in our English versions of the Bible—is the best regarded as a literal 24-hour day. Hence, when the Bible states that all things came about in the six literal days of creation, this would have included dinosaurs. In addition, human beings would have been created at virtually the same time as dinosaurs.

## Summary of Young-Earth Claims

1. Dinosaurs were created in the first week of creation along with human beings.

2. There was no death and no extinction of species before the first sin.

3. Dinosaurs coexisted with man.

4. The radiometric dating of dinosaur fossils cannot be trusted because these dating techniques cannot be trusted.

5. Dinosaurs entered Noah's ark along with the other creatures of the earth.

6. Ancient artwork gives evidence that dinosaurs coexisted with humans.

7. Dinosaurs are mentioned in the Bible.

One of the strong points of the young-earth position is the fact that an all-powerful Creator God certainly *could* have created the universe in six literal days. Such an all-powerful God has also left evidence of His existence in His creation (Romans 1:20)—whether this creation took place over a very short period or a very long one.

Hence, it is critical to take into account widely accepted scientific knowledge from experts, many of whom today are committed Christians and are in the position to know the facts.* The evidence that science observes in God's creation—when that evidence is

---

* See *Why Are Scientists Turning to God?* in the Examine the Evidence series. The author urges careful examination of any claims that contradict the larger body of current scientific evidence and knowledge.

properly interpreted—must be consistent with His miraculously given text, the Bible, and the account of creation that is given in it (see page 24).

## The Old-Earth Viewpoint

This point of view holds that the universe is about 15 billion years old and that the earth is about 4.6 billion years old—just as the larger body of science currently proposes. Furthermore, it believes that this is consistent with the text of the Bible when it is carefully considered in light of the latitude offered by the original Hebrew language. As mentioned, the word "day" in Genesis 1 is the word *yom* in Hebrew (for example the holiday *Yom* Kippur means "*day* of atonement"). However, *yom* can designate either a single 24-hour day, or any closed-end period of time. Thus the "days" were six closed-end periods of time—sometimes very long periods of time, such as hundreds of millions of years—which makes the account in Genesis entirely consistent with the scientific record.

### The Hebrew Word *Yom*

At the time of Moses, who wrote the Genesis account, there was no alternative Hebrew word available to indicate a closed-end period of time other than *yom*. Thus, if the inspired meaning of the Bible was pointing to six separate periods of time (epochs or eras), the word *yom* would have to have been used. The young-earth viewpoint holds that the inclusion of the words "evening" and "morning" after each day stresses the intended 24-hour meaning of the words. However, there are two problems with this conclusion. First, evening to morning is not 24 hours. Second, the Hebrews are well-known for the use of metaphors, and this could be an example of that. For instance, another possible metaphorical usage of the word "day" *(yom)* comes in Exodus 20:11, when the Sabbath "day" is related to the creation "day." Again, we should keep in mind there was no alternative word in Hebrew, other than *yom,* to indicate a closed-end period of time, whatever its duration.

## Summary of Old-Earth Claims

1. Dinosaurs were created about 248 million years ago.

2. Dinosaurs became extinct about 65 million years ago.

3. Dinosaurs were extinct long before humans were created.

4. The radiometric dating of fossils can be trusted because of the reliability of these techniques.

5. Dinosaurs were extinct long before Noah's ark was built.

6. Fossils give evidence that dinosaurs were long extinct before humans.

7. Dinosaurs are not specifically mentioned in the Bible.

The most significant aspect of the old-earth viewpoint is that it agrees with the scientific record. God's revealing of Himself through His creation—as observed by science—is every bit as significant as His more specific revealing through His written Word. And the two must be consistent.

# Dinosaurs—and How God Reveals Himself

## Special Revelation

Those who accept the Bible as the inspired, written Word of God consider it His special revelation to human beings. As such, every word of the Bible is important, and the Genesis account is regarded as fact. Where do the dinosaurs appear in the account of creation? As a separate group of creatures...they don't.

This may seem surprising. After all, seed-bearing plants are mentioned. Birds are mentioned. Creatures of the sea (fish) are mentioned. Livestock is mentioned, as are other creatures that move along the ground. Why not dinosaurs? Their very size alone, along with the impact they must have had during the time of their existence, would seem to warrant a "listing" in the Bible, wouldn't it?

The Bible is a special revelation to mankind. It deals with the relationship of human beings with God and teaches us through historical example. Therefore, it would not be surprising if all living things mentioned in the Bible were plants and creatures that had a *direct impact on humans,* be it in regard to food, clothing, or shelter. Dinosaurs apparently served no immediate purpose for mankind. Further, if dinosaurs were long extinct before the creation of human beings, they would never have had any direct contact with people.

## General Revelation

God also reveals Himself through His creation. As the psalmist writes, "The heavens declare the glory of God" (Psalm 19:1). Paul confirms general revelation in Romans 1:20: "Since the creation of the world God's invisible qualities—his eternal power and divine nature—have been clearly seen, being understood from what has been made." Therefore, when we encounter God's glory through His creation, we should reverence Him for this as well. The magnificence of the dinosaurs is obvious, as evidenced by the fossil record—regardless of when they were created and regardless of why. We can also be certain that God's general revelation of Himself through dinosaurs is consistent with the specific revelation that He has provided us in the Bible.

# Dinosaurs and Dating Techniques

Dinosaur fossils are dated using radiometric methods based on the rocks in which they are found. In some cases the fossils are embedded in rock that can be radiometrically tested. In other cases, upper and lower boundaries can be set for the age of the fossils because they are between layers of testable rock.

**Dating Dinosaurs Using Boundaries**

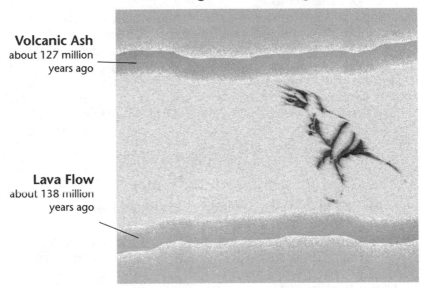

**Volcanic Ash**
about 127 million years ago

**Lava Flow**
about 138 million years ago

## Radiometric Dating

Because radiometric dating provides the major means of estimating the age of rocks and the fossils in or near them, let's look at it a little more closely. There are more than 40 types of radiometric dating, but all of them use essentially the same technique to examine rocks with radioactive elements. The number of daughter atoms present (those produced by radioactive decay) are measured in proportion to the number of parent atoms remaining (those that still have their original radioactivity). These are known as half-life measurements. The number of parent atoms decreases exponentially at each point in time.[3]

The accuracy of radiometric dating is very high. The half-lives of most radioactive isotopes used for dating are known to within plus-or-minus 2 percent. (It is critical for accuracy that the right method of dating is used for the right material. When anomalies appear, materials are often retested using a different method to check for agreement.)

Some of the kinds of events that radiometric dating is best at determining are, for instance, the time that has passed since the cooling of molten lava from a volcano; the end of a period of metamorphic heating (in particular, heating to greater than 1000 degrees); or the time since the death of a living creature (in this case, carbon dating is generally used). And recently, methods have been deployed that can be used to date even certain types of sedimentary rock. This is critical because many dinosaur fossils are found in this kind of rock.

## The Reliability of Radiometric Dating

The vast body of science accepts radiometric dating as reliable. In fact, several hundred laboratories around the world are actively using radioactive-dating methods. For instance, in the year 2001, more than a thousand articles on radiometric dating were published in recognized scientific journals. Hundreds of thousands of dates have been measured and published in the last 50 years— and when it was appropriate to corroborate these dates using different methods, very precise agreement in the measurements was found.

Sometimes the accuracy of radiometric dating is questioned because of anomalies that occasionally occur. It's then suggested that the entire methodology is flawed. This would be like claiming that penicillin doesn't work at all just because some patients are allergic to it. However, in such a case, penicillin might be the incorrect drug for a certain individual. A doctor would then prescribe an appropriate drug for that patient. Likewise, a particular dating method might be the wrong one for a specific situation or type of material. A researcher would then retest the material using the correct dating method.*[4]

## Dinosaurs on Pottery

Early Peruvian pottery has been found that seems to depict dinosaurs, including the triceratops, stegosaurus, and pterosaurus.[5] Is this evidence that they coexisted with humans there at the time the pottery was created?

Many believe that such artwork is nothing more than decoration—done by a culture that commonly honored creatures in various rituals. We know that ancient people found fossils, and like today, imaginatively re-created creatures of the past (see pages 6–9). In such cases, the drawings would be nothing more than depictions of what the fossilized bones were believed to represent.

---

* The author encourages anyone who has concerns about the reliability of radiometric dating to read *Radiometric Dating: A Christian Perspective* by Dr. Roger C. Wiens. For further information, see page 47.

   *Note of caution:* Some Web sites contain inaccurate or outdated information about radiometric dating. For a list of reputable sources, see Dr. Wiens' Web site (information on page 47).

# Biblical Questions About the Dinosaur Timeline

The dating of dinosaurs has raised some theological concerns.

- *Young-earth position*—Dinosaurs roamed the earth during human existence and *after* Adam's sin, perhaps 10,000 years ago.

- *Old-earth position*—Dinosaurs roamed the earth from about 248 million years ago to about 65 million years ago, when they became extinct—long before the creation of humans and therefore *before* Adam's sin.

Does the acceptance of an old-earth viewpoint contradict scriptural claims that there was no death before the original sin? For instance:

> Christ has indeed been raised from the dead, the firstfruits of those who have fallen asleep [died]. For since death came through a man, the resurrection of the dead comes also through a man (1 Corinthians 15:20-21).

> Sin entered the world through one man, and death through sin, and in this way death came to all men, because all sinned (Romans 5:12).

> The wages of sin is death (Romans 6:23).

Is a broad interpretation of "death" in these passages correct? In each case, death is *specifically related to human beings,* not to all of creation. Additionally, "death" might be more precisely defined as *spiritual* death, or separation from God. Thus, the death of dinosaurs prior to the creation of man would not create a problem or contradiction.

Let's also consider a simple biological analysis. God created a world in which at least plants were designed to be food (Genesis 1:29-30). Biologists know that every cell, including those of plants, is a complete living entity. Therefore, even in the garden of Eden before the first sin, when Adam and Eve were eating food, they were killing cells of life. Furthermore, a necessary part of maintaining a healthy body is the continuous process of cells dying and being replaced by healthy cells. But God pronounced His creation "good"—a creation which required a kind of death (in plants as a source of food, and in animal cells to maintain a healthy body). Therefore, not all death is bad; instead it depends on its context.

Lastly, would God calling His creation "very good" (Genesis 1:31) be contradicted by the existence of a world of dinosaurs tearing each other apart for food? No. We should not connect the actions of animals to God's expectations of human beings—who are creatures with a spirit, made by God in His image.

# Were Dinosaurs on Noah's Ark?

The old-earth timeline proposes, of course, that dinosaurs were long gone by the time humans were created, and therefore they were not on Noah's ark. For the young-earth timeline, the question of whether or not dinosaurs were on the ark has to be faced because of the obvious issue—the size of the creatures. There are three primary suggestions:

1. The dinosaurs, for whatever reason, became extinct before the flood.

2. The dinosaurs became extinct during the flood.

3. The dinosaurs were somehow taken onto the ark only to become extinct later.

## Extinction During the Flood

Though the first option is obviously not relevant to the ark or flood, the second option is interesting because of the many fossil graveyards that are found in various locations all over the earth.[6] In these graveyards, animals of all types, including species from many different geographic regions, are found mixed together in a single site. For instance, in the Gobi desert, more than two dozen theropod dinosaurs were found, along with some 200 mammals. Other graveyards have been found in New Mexico, Wyoming, Canada, Tanzania, Belgium, and Mongolia.

Of particular interest is a vast phosphate area covering some 40 square miles near Charleston, South Carolina. Throughout this large area, many fossils have been found, including those of pleiosaurs, sharks, rhinos, horses, mastodons, mammoths, porpoises, elephants, pigs, dogs, and even humans. (Some scientists holding the old-earth viewpoint have proposed various "mixing mechanisms" to explain this phenomenon.) Some dinosaur fossils have been found that even appear to be in a "swimming" position. This certainly seems to indicate their destruction in a flood, if not *the* flood.

# Dinosaurs on Board?

Could the dinosaurs really have been taken upon the ark? The vast majority of animals are insects and other very small creatures. With dinosaurs, however, we have a problem. Fully grown adult dinosaurs just wouldn't fit.

Take, for example, just the brachiosaurus. It stood 40 to 50 feet tall. The entire height of Noah's ark was 45 feet (Genesis 6:15), and presumably the support beams, roof, and keel shape of the ark would have reduced the available height substantially. So even if one were to assume that holes were cut through all decks from the bottom to the top, the brachiosaurus wouldn't fit.

## Calculating the Space

If we consider the floor area of the ark, this just reinforces the problem. The ark was very large—450 feet long by 75 feet wide, with each floor being 10 feet high (less the height of floors and support beams). However, this space would be quickly consumed by about 800 dinosaur species—many of which exceed the available height and average space. For example, the supersaurus was about 138 feet long and 54 feet tall; the ultrasaurus, about 100 feet long and 50 feet tall; the diplodocus, about 90 feet long and 17 feet tall; and the tyrannosaurus, about 40 feet long and 20 feet tall. In fact, unlike the many nondinosaur species of the world, *most* dinosaurs would be classified as extremely large. (Only a very few were in the 3- to 6-foot height range.)

Some 1600 dinosaurs (800 times two) would have needed to fit on a floor area of 33,750 square feet. (This assumes that one of three floors was devoted to dinosaurs, another floor was devoted to food and waste, and another floor was devoted to all the other creatures of the world, along with Noah's family.) With such a plan, each dinosaur would be allotted only 21 square feet (or a space of 4.6 feet by 4.6 feet).

However, we already have seen that quite a few dinosaurs approach or even exceed 100 feet in length—20 times longer than the allotted side dimension. Even medium-size dinosaurs (such as the allosaurus, spinosaurus, baryonyx, corythosaurus, triceratops, and many others) are from 30 to 60 feet long—6 to 12 times the allotted side dimension. They could simply not have fit into the allotted space.

## Would Babies or Eggs Have Solved the Problem?

In light of what we've just seen, it seems reasonable to suggest that baby dinosaurs were taken aboard taken the ark. After all, the reptiles of today have a slow metabolism and a growth rate slower than other animals, such as mammals. So, conceivably, they would be still small after their one-year voyage on the ark had passed.

Researchers who have studied the metabolism of dinosaurs have discovered, however, that it differs substantially from the metabolism of today's reptiles. In fact, they have concluded that dinosaurs had a metabolic growth rate similar to that of mammals.[7] Most mammals reach 100 percent of their full growth within a year. Hence, boarding baby dinosaurs would not solve the space problem inside the ark. The only solution would be if God had provided a special state of suspended growth through hibernation during the period of the flood. In this case, the baby dinosaurs would still have needed to have enough size and strength to have been self-sufficient at the time they boarded the ark.

Another suggestion is that no dinosaurs—only dinosaur eggs—were taken aboard the ark. This would resolve the size issue (assuming the eggs could be kept viable without hatching). But would this be consistent with the biblical record? Genesis 7:8-9 records that "pairs of clean and unclean animals, of birds and of all creatures that move along the ground, male and female, *came to Noah* and entered the ark, as God had commanded Noah." The Bible doesn't say that Noah went out to collect eggs, but that the creatures *came to him.*

To conclude, unless we make a special allowance for the dinosaurs—assuming either a unique hibernation caused by God, or that they were carried in egg form only—it appears that no dinosaurs were on the ark.

## Location of Mount Ararat, Resting Place of Noah's Ark.

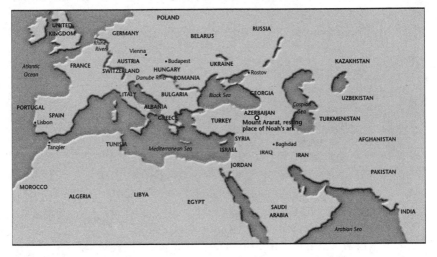

# Was the "Behemoth" a Dinosaur?

The book of Job is believed to be the oldest book in the Bible. Job is thought to have lived in the region of Mesopotamia (in what we call Iraq today). In this book, a curious creature is referred to—one that some people believe is a dinosaur.

> Look at the behemoth,
> which I made along with you
> and which feeds on grass like an ox.
> What strength he has in his loins,
> what power in the muscles of his belly!
> His tail sways like a cedar;
> the sinews of his thighs are close-knit.
> His bones are tubes of bronze,
> his limbs like rods of iron.
> He ranks first among the works of God,
> yet his Maker can approach him with his sword.
> The hills bring him their produce,
> and all the wild animals play nearby.
> Under the lotus plants he lies,
> hidden among the reeds in the marsh.
> The lotuses conceal him in their shadow;
> the poplars by the stream surround him.
> When the river rages, he is not alarmed;
> he is secure, though the Jordan should surge
>     against his mouth.
> Can anyone capture him by the eyes,
> or trap him and pierce his nose?
> —Job 40:15-24

Most study Bibles and commentators suggest that the word "behemoth" refers to an elephant or hippopotamus. Around the time of Job, the hippopotamus was revered as an intimidating and awesome creature in ancient Egyptian artwork. Some, however, believe "behemoth" refers to a dinosaur. Let's look at the options:

## What Is a "Behemoth"?

| Characteristic | Brachiosaurus | Elephant | Hippopotamus |
|---|---|---|---|
| 1. Feeds on grass | Yes | Yes | Yes |
| 2. Strength in loins | Yes | Yes | Yes |
| 3. Power in muscles of belly | Yes | Yes | Yes |
| 4. Tail sways like a cedar | Yes | No | Yes (see insert) |
| 5. Thigh sinews are close-knit | Yes | Yes | Yes |
| 6. Strong bones | Yes | Yes | Yes |
| 7. Strong limbs | Yes | Yes | Yes |
| 8. Lies under lotus plants | No* | Not Likely | Yes |
| 9. Hidden in marsh reeds | No* | Occasionally | Yes |
| 10. Concealed by lotuses | No* | Occasionally | Yes |
| 11. Surrounded by poplars by a stream | No* | Occasionally | Yes |
| 12. Lives in river | No* | Occasionally | Yes |

* It was once believed that the large sauropods—like the brachiosaurus—lived in the rivers to support their great weight. It has since been determined that, in fact, they were fully terrestrial, residing in forests and feeding on the tops of trees.

Apart from the above chart, other facts lead many commentators to believe that the hippopotamus best fits the characteristics of behemoth. The hippopotamus is an enormously powerful creature that was almost impossible to capture. Local peoples would hunt it for food because one kill could feed many people for a long period of time. Accounts of some of these hunts tell of ferocious resistance that, in many attempts, resulted in failure and death.[8]

### A Tail that "Sways Like a Cedar"

This phrase in Job 40 causes many to conclude that the behemoth could be neither an elephant nor a hippopotamus—both of which have short tails that certainly don't look much like a tall cedar tree. It is important to note, however, that the reference is not to the *size* of the tail, but to its *motion*. The tail is said to *sway* like a cedar, not to be as long as a cedar.

The curly tail of the elephant does not sway like a cedar. But the tail of the hippopotamus is rather straight and rigid, with a tuft on the end. Hence, when the hippopotamus moves its tail, there is a swaying effect that is indeed like that of a cedar.

# Was the "Leviathan" a Dinosaur?

There are several references in the Bible to a "leviathan." In all cases it seems to indicate a fierce water-based creature (or is a general term referring to family of marine monsters, or dragons). Some argue that the leviathan was a dinosaur. A complete description is given in Job 41 (emphasis is added to certain important characteristics):

Can you pull in the leviathan with a fishhook or tie down his tongue with a rope? Can you put a cord through his nose or pierce his jaw with a hook? Will he keep begging you for mercy? Will he speak to you with gentle words? Will he make an agreement with you for you to take him as your slave for life? Can you make a pet of him like a bird or put him on a leash for your girls? Will traders barter for him? Will they divide him up among the merchants? *Can you fill his hide with harpoons or his head with fishing spears?* If you lay a hand on him, you will remember the struggle and never do it again! Any hope of subduing him is false; the mere sight of him is overpowering. No one is fierce enough to rouse him. Who then is able to stand against me? Who has a claim against me that I must pay? Everything under heaven belongs to me.

I will not fail to speak of *his limbs, his strength* and his graceful form. Who can strip off his outer coat? Who would approach him with a bridle? Who dares open the doors of his mouth, ringed about with his *fearsome teeth?* His back has *rows of shields tightly sealed together; each is so close to the next that no air can pass between.* They are joined fast to one another; they cling together and cannot be parted. *His snorting throws out flashes of light;* his eyes are like the rays of dawn. *Firebrands stream from his mouth; sparks of fire shoot out. Smoke pours from his nostrils* as from a boiling pot over a fire of reeds. His breath sets coals ablaze, and flames dart from his mouth. *Strength resides in his neck;* dismay goes before him. The folds of his flesh are tightly joined; they are firm and immovable. *His chest is hard as rock,* hard as a lower millstone. When he rises up, the mighty are terrified; they retreat before his thrashing. The sword that reaches him has no effect, nor does the spear or the dart or the javelin. *Iron he treats like straw and bronze like rotten wood.* Arrows do not make him flee; slingstones are like chaff to him. A club seems to him but a piece of straw; he laughs at the rattling of the lance. *His undersides are jagged potsherds, leaving a trail in the mud* like a threshing sledge. He makes the depths churn like a boiling caldron and stirs up the sea like a pot of ointment. Behind him he leaves a glistening wake; one would think the deep had white hair. Nothing on earth is his equal—a creature without fear. He looks down on all that are haughty; he is king over all that are proud.

Other references to the leviathan in the Bible seem to be to a family of creatures—generally whales, crocodiles, or other great sea creatures.* The animal described in Job 41 is probably the great crocodile of the Nile. (This fearsome reptile is in the same class as a dinosaur—see chart on page 10.) Here are some reasons why the Nile crocodile fits the description:

- It lives in the region where Job lived.

- It is incredibly fierce and quick.

- It has a hide tough enough to repel harpoons and spears.

- It has short, very strong limbs.

- It has fearsome teeth.

---

* Other references are found in Job 3:8; Psalm 74:14; Psalm 104:26; and Isaiah 27:1.

- It has a strong neck.

- It has tough, impenetrable scales on its chest.

- It can easily snap strong items in its jaws.

- It has jagged bony protrusions underneath that would leave a trail in the mud.[9]

So the description seems to fit—with the exception of smoke and fire from its mouth and nostrils. "Smoke" might be explained by the appearance of the crocodile's breath on a cold morning. "Fire," however, is another issue—one that would need to be further considered in the case of either a crocodile or a dinosaur.

One possible explanation of the references to fire and flames might come from the legends that were prevalent in that general region. For example, great numbers of crocodile skeletons (combined with other dragon-like prehistoric skulls and bones) were collected and placed in shrines in both mountainous and low-lying regions of India on the border of China. Or for another example, about A.D. 220 the Greek historian Philostratus compiled a biography of Apollonius (about 265 B.C.), whose lost letters and manuscripts recounted fantastic stories of local people using magic to lure dragons out of the ground to pry precious gems from their skulls. The tales of these mystical creatures spoke vividly of great noise, fierce fighting, and their "flashing out every hue" from their skulls.[10]

Perhaps the most important feature in identifying the "leviathan" in Job as a Nile crocodile is the fact that the crocodile was regarded as fierce and virtually undefeatable. It grew to a length of some 30 feet, and had the ability to sneak up and suddenly snatch even lions from the banks of the Nile. The crocodile was depicted in much artwork throughout Egypt; in fact, it was venerated in the region. Interestingly, it was often displayed alongside the hippopotamus, which as discussed previously, was probably the behemoth in Job 40.

# Were "Dragons" in the Bible Dinosaurs?

Most references to "dragons" in the Bible are in the book of Revelation and are symbolic. Seemingly, they have nothing to do with dinosaurs.

However, if we take a closer look at the idea of dragons in the past, we find that their existence was commonly accepted, especially in China, where they were often depicted in artwork as long ago as 2000 B.C. They may have been composite creatures envisioned from ancient dinosaur fossils combined with extinct fossilized crocodiles. (As we noted, these bones were often found clustered together along the foothills of the Himalayas near China.)[11] The fierce crocodiles that were common in the region of China and throughout the entire Mediterranean probably added to dragon lore—and may have been considered a class of dragons in themselves.

The Greek word for "dragon"—*drakoon* (the word that is used in the New Testament)—literally means a "large serpent." Some scholars believe the concept was based on the large anaconda snake, which was often found in the desert or the wilderness. The word "dragon" was also extended to include many fanciful ideas that were not recorded as having been observed, but rather had been imagined. Specific characteristics that were attributed to the "dragon" were

- vast size

- something like a beard or dewlap

- three rows of teeth

- black, red, or yellow or ashy color

- a wide mouth

- respiration that could draw in birds flying over it

- a terrible hiss

- occasionally, feet and wings or a lofty crest[12]

The word "dragon" in Revelation undoubtedly refers symbolically to Satan, and parallels the description of the serpent in the garden of Eden.

## "Dragon" in the Old Testament

References to dragons in the Old Testament (the Hebrew Bible) are translations of the Hebrew words *tinniyn* or *taniyn*. These words are literally rendered "serpent," and "serpent" was understood by the ancients to mean some sort of sea monster, whale, or crocodile. When the Hebrew word *tinniyn* was translated into Greek by the Hebrew scholars who made the Septuagint translation around 250 B.C., the same word we've already seen was used: *drakoon*. Since ancient people often envisioned imaginary monsters, we cannot know whether the dragons mentioned in the Old Testament were real creatures or strictly symbolic references. Here are some appearances of the word "dragon" in the Old Testament:

> And I went out by night by the gate of the valley, even before the *dragon* well, and to the dung port, and viewed the walls of Jerusalem, which were broken down, and the gates thereof were consumed with fire (Nehemiah 2:13 KJV).

> Thou shalt tread upon the lion and adder: the young lion and the *dragon* shalt thou trample under feet (Psalm 91:13 KJV).

> In that day the LORD with his sore and great and strong sword shall punish leviathan the piercing serpent, even leviathan that crooked serpent; and he shall slay the *dragon* that is in the sea (Isaiah 27:1 KJV).

> Awake, awake, put on strength, O arm of the LORD; awake, as in the ancient days, in the generations of old. Art thou not it that hath cut Rahab, and wounded the *dragon?* (Isaiah 51:9 KJV).

Nebuchadrezzar the king of Babylon hath devoured me, he hath crushed me, he hath made me an empty vessel, he hath swallowed me up like a *dragon*, he hath filled his belly with my delicates, he hath cast me out (Jeremiah 51:34 KJV).

Speak, and say, Thus saith the Lord GOD; Behold, I am against thee, Pharaoh king of Egypt, the great *dragon* that lieth in the midst of his rivers, which hath said, My river is mine own, and I have made it for myself (Ezekiel 29:3 KJV).

## Dragons—or Bones?

In his writings about the region of India bordering China, the historian Philostratus (about A.D. 220) related that "no mountain ridge was without one [a dragon]." However, the basis for his remark was apparently the existence of many temples that contained crocodile skeletons along with prehistoric dinosaur skulls— including the skull of the fossilized giraffokeryx, which had a menacing dragon-like appearance.[13] For example, one Buddhist holy place located north of Taxila was referred to as "the shrine of the thousand heads."

Some of the prehistoric dinosaur skulls that were discovered had multiple horns and other outgrowths that look similar to the dragon heads that appeared in Chinese artwork.[14] And as we've already seen, the entire region of the Mediterranean was also rich in fossils, which were often depicted in artwork as ancient heroes and monsters (see pages 6–9).

To sum up, whether or not a "dragon" refers to a dinosaur is uncertain. Whether or not dragons are real or imaginary is uncertain. Paleontology suggests that the dragons in the Bible may be references to mythical monsters, which were conceived from crocodiles combined with extinct dinosaur fossils, rather than encounters with actual living dinosaurs.

# Conclusions

While we can't be sure what God had in mind with dinosaurs, we can be certain that He placed them on earth at one time in history as part of His loving provision in creation. Furthermore, we know that dinosaurs have nothing to do with the salvation that God has graciously offered to human beings.

Here are some specific points we've looked at:

1. Dinosaurs did not exist in the Roman Empire during the general time of Jesus (about 44 B.C. to A.D. 100). Evidence indicates that study of dinosaur fossils was already flourishing in the region at this time, even among such leaders as Caesar Augustus and Tiberius Caesar.

2. Dinosaurs did not exist in the time of the prophets (about 700 to 400 B.C.). Many fossilized bones were misidentified as mythological monsters and human heroes.

3. Dinosaurs did not exist during the time of Moses (about the time of the Trojan War, around 1250 B.C.). As later, dinosaur bones were often thought to be magical and from heroes of the past.

4. Dinosaurs did not exist at the time of Abraham and Job. Rather, bones of extinct crocodiles and dinosaurs were being used to create stories of dragons in the Mediterranean region.

5. Dinosaurs are not specifically mentioned in the Bible.

Why are dinosaurs not included in the Bible? Nobody knows for sure. God has no obligation to tell us. But it's interesting to note that all the creatures mentioned in the Bible have some specific role to play for human beings. Dinosaurs, apparently, had no role to play in interacting with people.

If, in fact, dinosaurs became extinct long before the creation of human beings, they may have had a critical part in *preparing* the earth for mankind. Consider that coal, oil, and natural gas have major importance for human civilization today. The generation of these fossil fuels required many years' accumulation of organic material. In order for this to occur, both plants and animals had to exist. Perhaps dinosaurs supplied much of the necessary carbon dioxide for the plants. Perhaps God even designed it that dinosaurs would become extinct in order to create a hidden provision that we could later unearth—thus revealing His glory in a most fascinating and dramatic way.

## Studying Creation

The Bible commands us to "test everything" and "hold onto the truth" (1 Thessalonians 5:21). Furthermore, in the Scriptures Jesus declares that the greatest commandment is to love God with all our heart, soul, *mind,* and strength (Mark 12:30). Loving God with our mind would include using our mind to understand His glorious creation and how He is revealed in it.

# How to Have a Personal Relationship with God

1. Believe that God exists and that He came to earth in the human form of Jesus Christ (see John 3:16; Romans 10:9).

2. Accept God's free forgiveness of sins and gift of new life through the death and resurrection of Jesus Christ (see Ephesians 2:8-10; 1:7-8).

3. Switch to God's plan for your life (see 1 Peter 1:21-23; Ephesians 2:1-7).

4. Expressly make Jesus Christ the Director of your life (see Matthew 7:21-27; 1 John 4:15).

## Prayer for Eternal Life with God

Dear God, I believe You sent Your Son, Jesus,
to die for my sins so I can be forgiven. I'm sorry for my sins,
and I want to live the rest of my life the way You want me to.
Please put Your Spirit into my life to direct me. Amen.

People who sincerely take these steps become members of God's family of believers. New freedom and strength are available through prayer and obedience to God's will. Your new relationship with God can be strengthened by

- finding a Bible-based church you like and attending regularly

- setting aside time each day to pray and read the Bible

- locating other Christians to spend time with on a regular basis

## God's Promises to Believers

*For Today*

Seek first his kingdom and his righteousness,
and all these things [that is, things that satisfy all your needs]
will be given to you as well
(Matthew 6:33).

*For Eternity*

Whoever believes in the Son has eternal life,
but whoever rejects the Son will not see life,
for God's wrath remains on him (John 3:36).

**Once we develop an eternal perspective, even
the greatest problems on earth fade in
significance.**

# Notes

1. Adrienne Mayor, *The First Fossil Hunters* (Princeton, NJ: Princeton University Press, 2000), p. 126.

2. <http://members.aol.com/paluxy2/sor-ipub.htm>. For an example of how evolutionists use cases like the Glen Rose footprints to create suspicion about biblical authority, see <http://www.darwin.ws/contradictions/paluxy.html>.

3. Roger C. Wiens, "The Dynamics of Dating—The Reliability of Radiometric Dating Methods," *Facts for Faith* newsletter, fourth quarter, 2001, pp. 11-18.

4. Chris Stassen, "The Age of the Earth," Talk.Origins archive: last updated April 27, 1997 (<http://www.talkorigins.org/faqs/faq-age-of-the-earth.html>).

5. <www.angelfire.com/mi/dinosaurs/dinocarving.html>.

6. <http://www.genesispark.com/genpark/grave/grave.htm>.

7. "Turbo-charged or Jump-Started? A Look at Dinosaur Metabolism" (<http://www.expandtheworld.com/html/dinosaur__metabolism_page_3.html>).

8. Job 40:15, Barnes' Notes, Electronic Database. Copyright © 1997 by Biblesoft.

9. Job 41:1, Barnes' Notes.

10. Mayor, p. 131.

11. Mayor, p. 130.

12. Bochart, *Hieroz.*, vol. 2. pp. 428-440; as cited in Revelation 12:3, Barnes' Notes.

13. Mayor, pp. 29-33.

14. <http://www.chinapage.com/dragon1.html>.

# References and Sources of Information
## General

Elwell, Walter A., ed. *Evangelical Dictionary of Theology*. Grand Rapids, MI: Baker Book House Co., 1984.

Farlow, James O., and Brett-Surman, M.K., eds. *The Complete Dinosaur.* Bloomington, IN: Indiana University Press, 1997.

<http://www.chelt.ac.uk/gdn/origins/life/ch2_3.htm>.

<http://www.chinapage.com/dragon1.html>.

<http://www.cs.colorado.edu/~lindsay/creation/punk_eek.html>.

<http://news.nationalgeographic.com/news/2002/05/0523_020523_rocks.html>.

<http://www.reasons.org>.

Mayor, Adrienne. *The First Fossil Hunters.* Princeton, NJ: Princeton University Press, 2000.

Youngblood, Ronald F. *New Illustrated Bible Dictionary*. Nashville, TN: Nelson, 1995.

Zodhiates, Spiros. *The Complete Word Study of the New Testament*. Chattanooga, TN: AMG Publishers, 1991.

Zodhiates, Spiros. *The Complete Word Study of the Old Testament*. Chattanooga, TN: AMG Publishers, 1994.

## The Dinosaur Timeline

*Young Earth*

DeYoung, Donald B. *Dinosaurs and Creation*. Grand Rapids, MI: Baker Book House Co., 2000.

<http://www.angelfire.com/mi/dinosaurs/deathsin.html>.

<http://www.answersingenesis.org/docs/4055.asp>.

"Are Dinosaurs Mentioned in the Bible?: Behemoth"
(<http://www.bibleandscience.com>).

<http://www.genesispark.org/genpark/park/park.htm>.

*Old Earth*

<http://www.educationplanet.com/articles/dinosaur.html>.

<http://www.expandtheworld.com/html/dinosaur__metabolism_page_3.html>.

<http://www.gospelcom.net/rbc/ds/q1112/q1112.html>.

<http://www.jpinstitute.com/news/jns_number_dino_species.jsp>.

<http://www.newswise.com/articles/2001/7/DINOSAUR.FSU.html>.

## Radiometric Dating

<http://www.asa3.org/ASA/resources/Wiens.html>.

<http://www.c14dating.com>.

<http://www.colorado.edu/INSTAAR/RadiocarbonDatingLab>.

<http://www.radiocarbon.com>.

Wiens, Roger C. *Radiometric Dating: A Christian Perspective*, rev. ed. 2002.

Dr. Wiens holds a PhD in physics, with a minor in geology. His doctoral dissertation was on the subject of isotope ratios in meteorites, including surface exposure dating. He was employed at the California Institute of Technology's Division of Geological and Planetary Sciences when he wrote the first edition of *Radiometric Dating* (1994; a revised version was written in 2002), and is presently employed in the Space and Atmospheric Sciences Group at the Los Alamos National Laboratory.

*Radiometric Dating* can be obtained by writing or e-mailing as follows:

Dr. Roger C. Wiens

941 Estates Drive

Los Alamos, NM 87544

RWiens@prodigy.net

It can also be found on the Internet, at

<http://www.asa3.org/ASA/resources/Wiens.html>.

Tough Questions—Quick, Factual,
Convincing Answers

# The Examine the Evidence Series
# by Ralph O. Muncaster

Are There Contradictions in the Bible?

Can Archaeology Prove the New Testament?

Can Archaeology Prove the Old Testament?

Can We Know for Certain We Are Going to Heaven?

Can You Trust the Bible?

Creation vs. Evolution:
What Do the Latest Scientific Discoveries Reveal?

Creation vs. Evolution VIDEO:
What Do the Latest Scientific Discoveries Reveal?

Dinosaurs and the Bible

Does Prayer Really Work?

Does the Bible Predict the Future?

How Do We Know Jesus Was God?

How Is Jesus Different from Other Religious Leaders?

How to Talk About Jesus with the Skeptics in Your Life

Is the Bible Really a Message from God?

Science—Was the Bible Ahead of Its Time?

What Is the Proof for the Resurrection?

What Is the Trinity?

What Really Happens When You Die?

Why Are Scientists Turning to God?

Why Does God Allow Suffering?